Kids Cooking

Students Prepare and
Eat Foods from
Around the World

George Ancona

CANDLEWICK PRESS

Today is cooking day! There are many smiles as the kids head to the kitchen. There they will learn how to cook healthy foods from all over the world. Every student puts on a name tag . . . not on the nose, Victor.

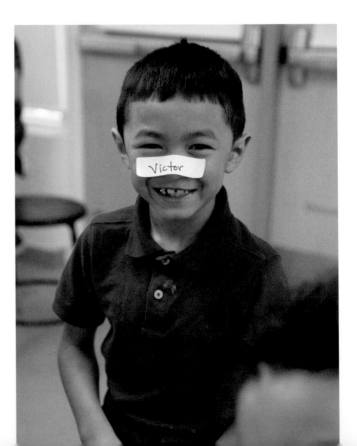

Ms. Linda, the cooking teacher, begins by talking about the root vegetables that they are going to cook today. She also shows the class a piece of fresh ginger root, which is a spice they will use.

The recipe is from Morocco, a country in North Africa. The spiced root vegetables will be served with a sauce called *chermoula* and oranges with mint leaves. Everyone must wash their hands before handling the food.

Ms. Jane shows Victor how to cut carrots safely with a butter knife. Natalie and the rest of the class chop sweet potatoes, carrots, parsnips, and turnips until the bowl is full.

Cutting a carrot

Alize measures the spices that are mixed with the vegetables. Then the teacher will roast the vegetables in the oven. The kids cannot handle anything hot.

While the teachers cook the veggies, the students draw pictures of the foods they have been chopping.

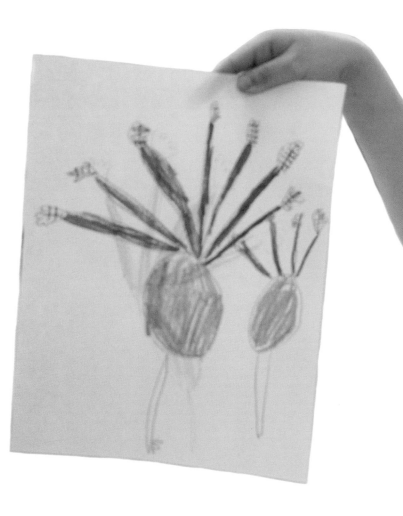

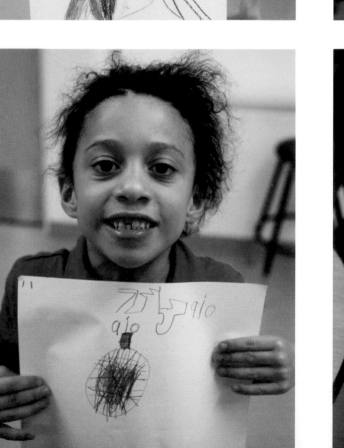

Esteban and Kimberley begin making the *chermoula* by chopping an herb called cilantro. Kimberley adds the spices, olive oil, and lemon juice.

Then, using a mortar and pestle, Natalie grinds everything into a smooth, delicious sauce. Natalie's dad lends a hand. Family members come to the kitchen to help on cooking days.

After washing the oranges, Nikolai and David peel and cut them. Alize and Anissah mix chopped mint leaves with the oranges.

When the veggies are ready, they are put on plates. Kimberley helps serve the colorful vegetables with *chermoula* and minted oranges.

Then comes the best part of the class. The happy kids
sit together to eat what they have made.

As-salamu alaykum means "Peace be upon you" in Arabic.

Today the kids will make Chinese-American fried rice with sweet and sour cucumbers. Chef Deb uses a globe to show the class where China is.

Rice is the main ingredient. It is mixed with zucchini, carrots, green onions, peas, ginger, cabbage, bok choy, eggs, soy sauce, and garlic.

While Chef Deb cooks the rice, Ezekiel and his classmates cut the vegetables. Chef Deb cooks the vegetables with garlic, ginger, and soy sauce. Then she mixes in the fluffy rice.

While the fried rice is being cooked, Zakary peels and slices cucumbers. Rice vinegar is mixed with water, sugar, and salt and poured over the cucumbers.

In China people use chopsticks to eat, but the kids here use forks.

Chī fàn luō means "Good eating" in Chinese.

After eating, cleanup time turns into silly time.

In Ms. Cathy's school kitchen, the kids are making a dish from Italy. Minestrone soup will be served with breadsticks.

Angel, Jacob, and Ely tear up green parsley, kale, and fresh thyme leaves before they add them to the pot.

They slice and chop garlic, onions, zucchini, carrots, and celery. Justin measures olive oil. It all goes into the pot along with chicken broth and white beans that Angel pours from a can. Then Ms. Cathy puts the pot on the stove to cook.

While the soup is cooking, the kids make breadsticks. Siena stirs in warm water, yeast, honey, olive oil, rosemary, salt, and whole wheat flour. Then Aubree pours in white flour.

Lily kneads the dough until it is stiff and smooth. Then she cuts the dough into pieces.

Each piece is rolled into a ball. Then the kids roll the dough balls into eight-inch-long breadsticks. Angel uses a ruler to measure her breadsticks. As Ms. Jane cooks the breadsticks, Elena brushes them with olive oil and Siena carefully sprinkles them with salt.

Ms. Jane brings the hot pot of minestrone to the table. She helps Ely stir the soup, then she ladles it into bowls for the class. Aubree sprinkles Parmesan cheese into each bowl. Then Siena and her classmates dig into their soup with their breadsticks.

Buon appetito means "Enjoy your meal" in Italian.

In another kitchen class, Ms. Bernadette places different kinds of tomatoes on a table so the kids can see and draw the various shapes. The kids are making salsa with the tomatoes.

Grape   Kumato

Vine Ripe   Roma

Antonio chops the tomatoes. Then chiles, garlic, red onions, lime juice, salt, pepper, and chopped cilantro leaves are added to the tomatoes.

The kids also make corn tortillas to eat with the salsa, a delicious combination from Mexico. The kids use a press to flatten each ball of dough into a tortilla. Then the tortillas are cooked.

tortillas

Ms. Emily spoons salsa into paper trays and adds a fresh, warm tortilla. Joaquin uses pieces of his tortilla to scoop up the salsa. He smiles as he eats. He is happy.

This class begins with a story about a family that loves to make and eat tamales.

There are three parts to a tamale: the dough, the filling, and the corn-husk wrapper. Ms. Annie and her students make the dough. After kneading it with their hands, they cut the dough into pieces and form little balls.

At another table the kids are making the vegetable filling. The filling is made with corn, zucchini, green chiles, and cheese.

The dough is pressed flat into the corn husk. Navaeh puts a spoonful of filling on top of the dough. The students learn to roll and fold the husks so that the tamale is tucked inside. Gabby ties the ends of the tamales with strips of corn husks.

The tamales are steamed in a big pot. When the tamales are ready, Ms. Annie spoons red chile salsa onto each dish with a tamale.

"Don't eat the corn husks, kids!" A mom helps everybody unwrap their delicious tamales.

Buen provecho means "Have a good meal" in Spanish.

corn Husks

chile sauce

chile

Masa

corn

Acknowledgments

This book would not exist if it hadn't been for the school kitchen doors that were opened by Jane Stacey and Anna Farrier of Cooking with Kids. They and their staff allowed me to watch, learn, and photograph for the book. I even got to taste what the kids made.

Thanks to Lynn Walters, who began the organization Cooking with Kids in 1995. Her goal was to introduce healthy food from around the world to children. It worked, and it keeps on working.

Thanks to my wife, Helga, who told me about the Cooking with Kids program that she had read about.

Thanks to the teachers from Cooking with Kids, who were not distracted by my photographing in their kitchens.

Thanks to the teachers and staffs of the schools I visited in Santa Fe, New Mexico:
Amy Biehl Community School
Cesar Chavez Community School
Gonzales Community School
Kearny Elementary School
R. M. Sweeney Elementary School
Turquoise Trail Charter Elementary School

Thanks to the young artists who made the wonderful drawings in this book.

Thanks to Roy McKeag, who always crosses the arroyo to help the author's computer behave.

Thanks to Stephan Wacks for his technical assistance.

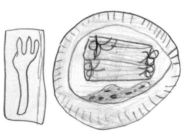

Find recipes at www.candlewick.com/kidscooking